Small Schools and Democratic Practice

by Clive Harber

Educational Heretics Press

Published 1996 by Educational Heretics Press
113 Arundel Drive, Bramcote Hills, Nottingham NG9 3FQ

British Cataloguing in Publication Data

A catalogue record for this book is available from the British
Library

ISBN   0-9518022-9-1

Design and production: Educational Heretics Press

Printed by Antony Rowe Ltd., Chippenham, Wiltshire.

Contents

Introduction

I would like to start with a brief educational autobiography.   My formal, state education began in a small primary school in south London.   It was small because it was new and on the day it opened only a dozen or so children attended and the numbers grew only gradually over the next few months.   For the rest of my stay at this school until I left at age eleven I was close to this cohort of children.   For the first year or two it was possible to know all the other children and the staff and on the whole I remember this period warmly.   Gradually the school became larger, less friendly and, under the influence of a very strict, cane-wielding head teacher, it became more competitive and more authoritarian.   This was a good preparation for my secondary education.

I went on to a selective 'grammar' school of about 850 students which has since become independent.   Here numbers were again such that it was just about possible to know a reasonable proportion of the other students and staff, especially as there was a developed house system which helped to cross-cut year and class groups.   However, the traditional curriculum and authoritarian teaching methods and school organisation were such that, had it not been for the fact that the majority of students were from a middle class background, and on a guaranteed conveyor belt to university, there would have been serious disaffection.   Among the minority of students from a working class background, of which I was one, there was indeed disaffection and alienation.   This expressed itself in various forms of deviance and even illegal behaviour, though in my case until the age of fifteen it largely resulted in boredom, lack of interest, mental truancy and coasting.   In the fifth year of this school, however, by sheer good fortune I found myself in classes taught by a clutch of new young teachers who were more approachable, had a sense of humour, knew their subject well and used slightly more participatory classroom teaching methods.   The looming threat of the 'O' level examination became more of a challenge and my subsequent discovery of the social sciences and critical debate in the sixth form, as an undergraduate and as a student teacher rescued my interest in education which had been seriously threatened by my experience of school.

My first teaching job was in a very large comprehensive school of 2,400 students. It was of course impossible to know more than a fraction of the students and more than a small proportion of the staff. It was often argued that the size of the school meant that we could offer a more diverse curriculum than other schools, which suited me as the school gave me the opportunity to develop as a politics and social science teacher in a way that the majority of other schools at the time could not. However, as I became more familiar with the bureaucratic and mass organisational nature of the school, the problems of communication (there was a tannoy system in each classroom on which the deputy head used regularly to interrupt lessons) and keeping track of students academically and pastorally became more obvious. Not surprisingly, the school also experienced considerable problems of truancy and deviance. I left the school less convinced about the arguments for economies of scale than when I had joined.

From 1980 to 1995 I was a lecturer in education at a large civic university in the British midlands. Like other major civic universities it is a very large organisation and it would be true to say that, despite various mission statements and corporate logos, I never really had any sense of what it meant to belong to the institution or of what the identity of the institution was - it was simply too big to identify closely with. I certainly knew very few colleagues from outside of my own Faculty. One indicator of this was the fact that for the last ten years I hardly ever bothered to read the university bulletin. It is difficult to be that interested in an institution with which you do not clearly identify. Even the School of Education in which I worked during that period had over 50 full-time academic members of staff, many part-time and temporary academic staff and many administrative and secretarial staff. As the School grew, and even though the decision-making structures had become more participatory, there were more and more staff that I neither recognised nor had any idea about what they did and I suspect that I was not alone in this. It was also impossible to know more than a fraction of the students.

I therefore welcome this opportunity to explore relationships between the size of educational institutions and the education that goes on inside them. I start with a strong belief in democratic education based on experience that has been expressed in many books and articles prior to this one. This gives me a certain predisposition towards smaller schools, but it is important both to recognise the real problems faced by small schools and how they might be mitigated or overcome and to ask how some larger schools have attempted to ameliorate the potentially harmful aspects of their size. I hope that this book goes some way towards achieving this.

Before exploring the debates surrounding small schools and democratic education it is first necessary to ask the question of what we mean by a 'small' school. This is, of course, an impossible question to answer in the end, as small schools exist in many different countries and their governments have different definitions of smallness. In Britain the definition has varied over time from 70 and under for a primary school to 400 for a secondary school, though recently the official figure for a small secondary school seems to have increased to between 600 and 900 (Richmond 1992). Bray (1987a:15) has a guideline of 100 students or less for a primary school and 180 students or less for a secondary school, though he notes that in some countries it is common to find primary schools with fewer than fifteen students and secondary schools with fewer than 60 students. The New Zealand government has set the official minimum size for a school at nine students whereas in Hong Kong one school has only four students but two teachers. In England in 1993 there were 9,500 primary schools with fewer than 200 students and about 3,500 with fewer than 100 (Webb 1993). Moreover, different writers on school size each have their own definitions. Francis (1992), for example, lists different studies of primary schools as defining smallness as 100, 125, 132, 441 and 475 students. We shall also see how the definition of smallness varies when individual schools are discussed in other parts of the book.

Clive Harber
University of Natal
June 1996

Chapter one

The School Size Debate

Both small and large schools have their advocates and their arguments will be reviewed in this chapter.   However, it is important to bear in mind that while some of the debate is factual and some is on the question of how best to achieve agreed outcomes, much of it is also based on values about the relative importance of various aims of education and the educational processes required to achieve them.   Here we shall organise this debate by taking each of the main arguments concerning small schools and examine the extent to which the case for or against is supported by evidence.

Costs

Perhaps the major argument against small schools is that they are too expensive to run.   This is certainly the reason put forward for the closure of many small rural schools in England and Wales, for example.   This argument is usually expressed in terms of larger schools having lower unit costs;   i.e. that it is cheaper to educate students of equivalent ages in a larger than a smaller school.   This is for two main reasons.   Firstly, because larger schools spread their fixed costs such as libraries, science and language laboratories and   buildings over more children, so the per capita cost is lower.   Secondly, large schools often have higher student:teacher ratios which result in a lower cost per student.   As teacher salaries typically account for 80% of a school's recurrent budget it is therefore important to use teachers efficiently and this means a higher student:teacher ratio.   Small is therefore economically inefficient.   Also, because small schools in rural areas absorb more educational resources, this also deprives urban children of better educational resources.

This argument is challenged on a number of grounds by those who favour small schools. Small schools do not necessarily have lower student:teacher ratios. It is quite possible that student and teacher numbers fit neatly and classes are full. As Bray (1987a:25/6) illustrates in his book, it is a question of thresholds, with costs only rising sharply when the number of students in the school means that it becomes necessary to employ a new teacher.

Moreover, the higher fixed costs of libraries and laboratories must be offset against other costs that accrue from closing small schools or building large ones. The first of these is travel. When distances to school are large, as they often are in rural areas, then the state must provide some form of transportation directly or provide travelling allowances for the families of the students concerned. A study carried out by Aston University, for example, found that in one rural area of Britain the local authority, having created a middle school of nearly 600 places in a small market town, found itself allocating - in 1983 - £45,000 for transport costs which would have gone a long way towards supporting the small village schools which had been closed (quoted in Stiles: 1986).

Also, in some countries without an adequate transport system it may even be necessary to provide boarding facilities, which are expensive. Moreover, in very large schools there is often a need to employ specialised administrative staff which adds to costs, and heads and deputy heads of larger schools not only tend to be more senior but are also paid more, simply because the school is larger. Thus, it is perhaps not surprising that careful studies of small schools (Galton and Patrick:1990; Tomlinson:1990) have suggested that the cost argument is inconclusive one way or another. Moreover, a study by Aberdeen University found that when such wider costs were taken into account out of fifteen schools that were closed in the 1970s in Scotland, eight made no difference to spending, for three the results were inconclusive and in four cases there were probably actually increases in costs (quoted in Stiles 1986).

Concentrating solely on costs also leaves out the other side of the financial equation - income. In many countries (especially, though not exclusively, in developing areas) schools have to rely heavily on resources contributed by the local community (see, for example, Bray with Lillis 1988). For a number of reasons small schools might find it easier to raise community resources. This is because small schools are physically closer to their communities so it is easier to identify with them and in small schools individual contributions are more likely to be noticed and appreciated. Moreover, village communities are usually aware that costs may be used as an argument against their school and are therefore keen to protect their school against closure by providing extra resources.

Cost Effectiveness and School Effectiveness

However, perhaps the strongest set of arguments against the cost criticism of small schools is that what must be considered is not just financial inputs, but the whole, and much wider, issue of cost effectiveness. This raises the question of the results of the financial investments made. Given that the evidence on costs is inconclusive, do small or larger schools provide better educational outcomes for the money invested? This argument concentrates on the processes of schooling - on what schools actually do to students. However, before examining these arguments in more detail it is important to note the point made by Meighan (1992:39) who accepts that both small and large schools can be ineffective but that,

> "If you maintain one highly ineffective school of one thousand pupils, you have a thousand person disaster. If the same pupils were divided into ten small schools of one hundred pupils each, it would require all ten to be highly ineffective to achieve the same level of disaster. The chances of this are not very high. Ten small schools are a better bet."

Those who argue in favour of small schools also argue that small schools are much less likely to be ineffective anyway. This is because the quality of relationships between staff and students and amongst students themselves is better in smaller rather than larger schools. The criticism of big schools is that they reflect a philosophy of education that has its origins in the second half of the nineteenth century with the beginnings of mass formal schooling. The idea was to provide enough education to produce literate and numerate workers who would then go on to take up subordinate roles both in the workplace and in the wider society. Indeed, the organisation of schools reflected this ideology of the mass production of workers becoming like factories or large commercial concerns in their bureaucratic organisational style and their emphasis on the 'economies of scale'. Commenting on the role of schools in modernisation, Shipman notes that,

> *"Punctuality, quiet orderly work in groups, response to orders, bells and timetables, respect for authority, even tolerance of monotony, boredom, punishment, lack of reward and regular attendance at place of work are the habits to be learned at school" (1971:54/55).*

The negative outcomes of this are emphasised by proponents of small schools. Toogood (1991:2/3), for example, argues that,

> *"This mass situation seems to require adherence to different qualities, such as conformity, ability to stick to a single line of thought, to carry out instructions without divergence, to act under instructions, etc. That is so far as the learner is concerned. So far as the teacher is concerned, the role in the large scale situation is quite different. A different sort of person is required to teach large groups in large, monolithic schools, someone who is a good bureaucrat, a good technocrat, who has a good battlefield presence, can command order, entertain large crowds and above all be pro-active and dominant, often autocratic. To my shame I think I also learnt how to do all that rather well. But it didn't make me a good teacher".*

Certainly, when the student's view of schooling is taken into account there is long-standing evidence of dissatisfaction with schooling, particularly secondary schooling (Meighan, 1986: Ch.3). A survey of 3,600 students in schools in Canada found widespread evidence of what Michael Fullan and his colleagues call 'the alienation theme'. For example, they found that,

- only a minority of students think that teachers understand their point of view and the proportion decreases with educational level
- less than one fifth of the students reported that teachers asked for their opinions and ideas in deciding what or how to teach
- principals and vice principals were not seen as listening to, or being influenced by, students
- substantial percentages of students, including one out of every two high school students, reported that 'most of my classes are boring' (Fullan, 1991:171).

What is clear from the research of Fullan and his review of the research of others is that students are consistently critical of a lack of communication, dialogue, participation and what he terms student 'engagement' in the processes of schooling. Generally the students exhibit little sense of identity or belonging.

This evidence of alienation and its attendant social dangers and risks has been consistently linked to the size of schools by those who advocate small schools. James Hemming, for example, argues that,

'Within the mass world of modern times, small groups do exist and thrive, but the overall intimacy has been lost, while personal isolation has become a constant risk for individuals. A scan of the human scene overall shows clearly that the quality of personal lives and the values of the social milieu are intricately interrelated, while both are conditioned by the degree of social intimacy that exists. This indicates that intimacy, not social massing, is the right climate for fostering human development and formative education. Hence the relationship that is found everywhere between expanding community size and social/personal degeneration: crime, alcoholism, drugs, stress, neurosis, loneliness and all the other outcomes of depersonalised mass society' (1991:8).

Heal (1978), for example, concludes that misbehaviour is more common in large primary schools than small primary schools. The need for smaller schools where students are not reshuffled every 40 or 80 minutes is also a theme of Etzioni's 'communitarian' agenda which has been widely discussed in centre left circles in the USA and Britain recently. The argument is that such fragmentary schooling hinders the development of strong relationships and bonds and is a contributory factor to vandalism, deviance and disaffection (Etzioni 1995).

One major review of the literature on effective schooling is also interesting in that it devotes some thirty-odd pages to a section on the 'perceived outcomes of secondary schooling' which focuses on 'disadvantaged and disaffected pupils' and 'discipline and disruption' (Reid, Holly and Hopkins, 1987). The evidence reviewed suggests this is much more than just perceived - so much so that they devote a whole chapter (7) to 'combating disaffection'. At the beginning of this chapter they argue that too many students do not identify or associate with their institutions and teachers and hence the prime requisite for combating student alienation is the need to make every student feel that he or she matters. It is when students feel unwanted, rejected, uncared for or disillusioned that they start manifesting their disaffection by staying away, disrupting lessons or underachieving. In this area, they argue, secondary schools could learn a great deal from their primary counterparts because in primary schools students feel a part of the school as if they were a member of a family and identify with their peers and teachers, whereas in many secondary schools some students soon feel lost. Perhaps, not surprisingly given this analysis, their review of the evidence from research on effective schools simply states that 'effective schools are likely to be smaller' (p.29).

Small schools, it is argued by their supporters, through the familiarity of strong, personal, and face-to-face relationships, drastically reduce this risk of alienation and isolation fostered by the impersonality of large schools and which contribute to the considerable social costs of vandalism, crime and general mental well being. One head teacher, for example, argues why this is so,

'Parents have long been suspicious of the large school. They rightly fear its anonymity. Most meetings in corridors are encounters with strangers. Pupils will do things when they are not known, to people whom they do not know, far more readily than they would to those whom they do know.

A large mass of teenagers in a teenage ghetto called a school produces its own adolescent mores....But the aim of a school is to inculcate more mature, adult attitudes. Every time a school gets bigger, the ratio of adults to pupils stays the same but the number of teenagers becomes more potent. Yet, if we are to attack the alienation of the young from our schools, they must feel that they belong in them....Love is a normal feature of families; charity replaces it in larger units. The large school is such a unit and resembles a city; it should be like a village. Otherwise it will continue to mirror our urban failure' (Anderson, 1991:13).

The same head teacher also makes the point that it is not only students that are affected by the mass production environment of large schools. He argues, amidst increasing general evidence of a rise in stress levels among teachers, that small schools help to reduce stress. He notes that he has worked in schools of 300, 600, 1,700 and 950 and that the first was by far the least stressful and gave the most job satisfaction because it was on a human scale, not a factory scale.

St. Paul's Community School in Birmingham is a small school of 25 students and was established by Dick Atkinson in the early 1970s specifically for those students who had been expelled from comprehensives in the city because of their record of truancy and troublesome behaviour.   Atkinson's argument is that small is beautiful - 'It is easy for pupils to get lost either within or outside a large school. In St. Paul's they are found. They are motivated by seeing the names of pupils who left a couple of years ago on the roll of honour'. The school has a relaxed atmosphere and students do not wear uniforms. One former student who had stopped attending his previous school and who was now planning to go on to study software engineering commented that 'It is very informal, the teachers will talk to you and you can communicate with them as people'. In 1994 43% of the GCSE entrants at St. Paul's gained five or more A-C grades, placing it sixth in the league table of the city's non-selective schools (*Independent* 16/2/94). If a so-called 'value added' approach had been taken it would no doubt have come at or near the top.

Thus, if we take into account the negative social consequences of large schools as costs, it can be strongly argued that it is they that are expensive, not small schools. Moreover, there is every sign that small schools can match or exceed bigger schools according to the more conventional and measurable 'output' indicators of school effectiveness. Tomlinson (1990), for example, did research into six small rural secondary schools in Warwickshire with less than 600 students on roll. He found that in terms of academic success the six schools either equalled or excelled larger schools in the county. The schools used exclusion and suspension markedly less than other schools and the majority of students enjoyed school with a higher proportion than average taking part in school or house sport.

Patrick and Hargreaves (1990) compared the English and mathematics performance of students in small primary schools with the performance of students in a study conducted seven years previously in larger suburban schools, and concluded that students from small schools appeared to perform no worse and in some respects better than those in the larger schools. Mortimore et al (1988) conclude from their study of school effectiveness during the junior school years that there is no evidence that larger schools are associated with better educational progress in any area.

Bray (1987a:34/5) also summarises research on educational achievement which suggests that small schools can provide as good as or even better quality education as large schools:

- A study in America covering 218 secondary schools with enrolments ranging from 18 to 2,287 found that the versatility and performance scores of students were consistently higher in small schools and that they reported more satisfaction and displayed more motivation in all areas of school activity (Campbell 1980).

- Analysis of the 1985 examination results in Alberta, Canada showed that 'pupils in small high schools (under 200 pupils) achieved at or near the provincial average, with some exceeding the average significantly'. The same was true at the primary level (Farrant 1986).

'There is no evidence whatsoever from surveys of attainment in Wales that the measured attainments of children in small rural schools are depressed' (Nash 1977).

However, it is also important to remember that 'effectiveness' can only really be judged in terms of goals and many of those who advocate small schools as preferable to large schools do so because they are aiming at more than just the conventional outcomes of schooling measured solely by examination results. They desire different sorts of people from those shaped by conventional schooling and in particular, they would argue, damaged by over-large schools. Smaller schools are not only as conventionally successful as large schools but have the potential to create more flexible, independent, co-operative, responsible and mature people. Philip Toogood, for example, describes an encounter with Harry Ree, the doyen of community educationalists in Britain, about Aneurin Bevan's statement that, 'The big is the enemy of the best' in terms of what was meant by the 'best' in education:

'I came to the conclusion that we were meaning, "the most creative", but that this creativity needed very close defining. When I am teaching now I pay particular attention to the appearance of three characteristics in my students. Fluency, Divergency of Thought and Originality. These three qualities of creativity seem to prosper best in situations where two or three people are gathered together, certainly where the number of people does not exceed single figures' (Toogood, 1991:2).

The reason put forward for this concerns the quality of the educational relationships that are possible in small schools - the processes of education - and this will be discussed in the next section on curriculum.

Curriculum

Curriculum is used here to describe not only what is taught but also how it is taught. It is also used in its broadest sense to encompass all that is learned in school, not just what appears on the timetable. Small schools are often accused of having a restricted curriculum and offering only a limited range of subjects. This is because they have fewer teachers and thus a smaller pool of talent and expertise. Also, group sizes in small schools may be such that the number of students for a subject is not viable and small schools may be restricted in terms of the sports they can offer.

However, this concept of curriculum is a very limited and a very subject-bound one and ignores the question of the roles of the teacher and students in curriculum provision. Much is now available, for example, through radio, television, postal correspondence courses, newspapers, magazines, computers, libraries, teachers' centres and video which enable a much more flexible approach to curriculum and learning. In this way, both through more independent forms of learning and through students being engaged in co-operative learning with each other, small schools can actually offer as diverse a curriculum as big schools. Moreover, because small schools are more like extended families and are less bureaucratic, rule-bound and regimented than large schools, they can use learning resources in a flexible, student-centred manner that better meets the need of the young person. These learning and teaching methods can be used to teach both a centrally prescribed and authoritarian national curriculum, such as the one in Britain, or a more decentralised, negotiated curriculum of the sort recently introduced, ironically, in Russia. Hopkins (1985) found little evidence that the limited range of staff expertise in a small school necessarily leads to a restricted curriculum. Indeed, Nash (1980) in his research on small schools in North Wales found that small schools had pioneered teaching methods - family grouping, integrated studies, individualised learning - recommended to large schools by advisers as good practice. As Hopkins and Ellis (1991) point out, while problems of teacher isolation, fewer career prospects and personality clashes between student and teacher do occur, these kinds of problems can be reduced or avoided and appear to become significant only when inadequate resources, negative attitudes and weak and inappropriate teaching occur - and these can cause problems in any school.

Moreover, even small rural schools in developing countries which are often (though not always) starved of commercially produced resources there is much that can still be done to provide a stimulating and relevant curriculum. This interesting and significant example is from Zimbabwe:

"In a remote school in Matabele land there was a young student teacher whose working conditions and social background were just as poor as that of any other student teacher and as that of the fifth grade children he was teaching. The children were busy doing different things. They seemed interested in what they were doing and smiled friendlily to us, the intruders. Often children in these remote areas used to stare at foreigners with a frightened look. Not so with these children. In one corner of the classroom there was a bookshelf made of old bricks and planks wrapped up in newspaper. There were a few booklets and some magazines which the teacher had collected together with the children. In the windows, some with broken panes, big seeds had been threaded on strings and were waving happily as decoration in the light breeze from the window. In one corner the organisation of SADCC was illustrated by means of empty coke tins and stones. Newspaper pictures were glued to the boxes, symbolising different SADCC departments. On the floor maps of different countries were shaped with pebbles. There was hardly an empty space on the mud floor. But children stepped carefully around the creations so as not to destroy them. In another corner was a "spelling tree" - just a few branches with cards hanging on strings like a Christmas tree. Children worked in pairs, asking each other to spell the difficult words. In another group some children were playing with a set of home-made maths cards. To honour the guests the children picked their self-made costumes from the hooks on the wall, one drummed and the others performed a joyful and very rhythmic dance. To teach children about traditional handicraft techniques, like how to build a proper hut or how to make a hob-kerry, elderly people from the village were invited to the school to share their wisdom and knowledge with the children" (Nagel, 1992:xviii).

Above all, however, for those who favour small schools, there is the quality of the relationship between students and between staff and students. In a smaller school teachers can get to know their students much better and understand their needs more effectively, and students can get to know each other much better. This allows each child's progress to be carefully monitored and discussed on a long term basis. As Munro (1975) claimed, 'By their very nature these schools are ideally suited to providing attention to individual differences, a principle which is at the heart of all good teaching'. Also, there will opportunities for children to learn from each other and to interact with different age groups as in a large family. Thus, because people in small schools know each other well and there can be a greater ease of communication, they usually have a more co-operative and positive atmosphere than in large schools. Three of the key aims of the Human Scale Movement which supports and promotes small schools are that education should,

- take place in groups small enough so that pupils and teachers can get to know each other well and thus feel valued, secure and supported

- be active rather than passive; children learn most effectively by talking, thinking, doing, in co-operation with others

- emphasise the importance of relationships between teachers, pupils, parents and with the environment (Human Scale Movement 1992).

Not only do children in small schools help each other more regularly out of necessity, but numerically they have a much better chance of joining in sporting and cultural activities such as school plays or concerts. Bray (1987a:32) quotes one researcher to the effect that,

> *"All the children, by necessity, must be given responsibilities and must contribute to discussions and assemblies. In larger schools these responsibilities tend to be given to the select few."*

Although it is often suggested that large schools provide a wide variety of social contacts, thereby creating more confident and mature people, those in favour of small schools argue that the opposite is more likely to be the case. What large schools actually provide, increasingly as children move from early primary to senior secondary school, is regular formal confinement with a group of people of the same age and in practice informal confinement with people of the same gender. Meighan (1992:42) makes the following comment,

> *"It comes as no surprise that both home-based educated children and those from small schools are constantly reported as being more socially mature than the products of such a system because of the flexibility of the social contacts they tend to provide. John Holt noted that whenever he made this point about the quality of social experience in large schools in discussions about education in the USA, he never encountered argument but sad-faced nods of agreement often followed by harrowing personal stories illustrating his analysis."*

Research tends to support this. Burstall (1974) investigated British primary school students' achievements in French. She followed the careers of 17,000 students over ten years and included small rural schools in her sample. She found not only that the test performance of the students in the small schools was consistently superior to that of the students in the large schools but that this was because the small schools tended to encourage co-operative behaviour and to lack the negative motivational characteristics of the competitive classroom in which success for the few can be achieved only at the expense of failure for the many.

Howells (1982) also found that there was no evidence that small schools were any less educationally viable than large schools. This study also found that students in small rural schools had a better attitude towards work and, having been accustomed to working on their own, could be given more responsibility for the organisation of their work.

Indeed, if smaller schools and smaller classes did not provide a reasonable curriculum and stand a better chance of producing better examination results and more confident students, it would be hard to explain why so many expensive private or independent schools feature their small size in advertisements and brochures in order to attract parents.

Small Schools and the Community

Another major argument in favour of small schools, especially in rural areas, is their very local, community-based nature. The importance of this is stated clearly in the philosophy of the Human Scale Movement,

> *"The present crisis in education should be addressed by moving in exactly the opposite direction to the big by decentralising institutions, devolving power, slowly dismantling large-scale systems and replacing them by smaller, more controllable, more efficient, people-sized units, rooted in local circumstances and guided by local citizens" (1986:1).*

Often when small schools in rural areas are closed the phrase used is that 'the heart has been torn out of the village'. Why can the school be so important to the local community? Unlike large towns, villages may have only one or a few centres of social interaction. The village school is, therefore, a more prominent and proportionately more important institution than a town school. It becomes a major focal point of village life. Parents chat outside the school gate, village meetings are held in the school and it is where people vote in local and national elections. Communications within a small locality are usually good, so that not only do teachers get to know their students' family backgrounds, but also relationships with parents are based on frequent informal discussions. Also, because of their education and links with the wider world, teachers in rural schools tend to play stronger leadership roles and contribute more to community development than they do in urban areas.

Moreover, if there is no village school there can be a tendency for parents to leave the area and move nearer to a school, thereby hastening the decline of that community.   One researcher examined population changes in Devon in the United Kingdom. The researcher looked at 400 communities which had records for the years 1911 to 1961. Among the communities, 287 had a school throughout the period while 113 had none. The study found that communities with a school grew on average by 2% during this period while those communities without a school declined by an average of 12%. Schools were not the only factor in this, but they played a major part (quoted in Bray, 1987a:19). It is not surprising, therefore, that the Schools Council in its **Small Schools Study** (1975) concluded that 'good small schools perform useful, sometimes essential, social and educational functions'.

The Issue of Choice

The issue of choice in education is one which has been at the centre of much political discussion in the 1980s and 1990s. As noted above, parents who can afford private schools for their children can exercise choice and when they do so they regularly see small as attractive. However, in many countries those without the necessary level of money are forced to accept what the state provides. In Britain, where the government has made much of the rhetoric of choice, there has in fact been a diminution of choice. Before the introduction of the national curriculum in 1988 there was a degree of curriculum decentralisation so that, although schools tended in practice to do much the same as each other, there was some difference and therefore at least some genuine choice. The introduction of a standardised national curriculum means that all schools are now much more similar in what they provide. The real 'choice' has become between which school is best at delivering the national curriculum - as was said about Ford motor cars in the early days of their production, you can have any colour as long as its black. Moreover, with the popular schools heavily over-subscribed it is more a case of the schools choosing the students than vice versa.

Real choice would involve parents and children being able to choose what of sort school they wanted. It certainly would not have resulted in the closing down of so many rural small schools. Edington and Gardner (1984), for example, conclude from a study of students attending 195 elementary schools in Montana that the students in small schools hold more positive attitudes towards school than their peers in larger schools. Edmonds and Besai (1977) report a similar finding in their comparison between 737 students in small schools and 987 students in large schools on Prince Edward Island. The study found that students in the smaller schools reported more satisfaction and less discontent with school. A survey of students in Britain, Canada and Australia also found that they were strongly in favour of small schools. Cohesiveness and satisfaction were seen as high and friction as low. Schoolchildren really liked their small schools and enjoyed being there, and for them it provided a desirable learning environment (Edmonds 1989). A study of 4,746 junior school children in one local education authority in Britain found that school size made a significant difference in attitude towards school, with children in the smaller schools recording a significantly more positive attitude. The author concludes that small schools seem to be generally happier places and argues that there is a number of studies which point to a positive relationship between student attitudes and progress in other educational areas (Francis 1992).

De la Cour (1988) describes how in Denmark parents are provided with a more genuine choice and small schools flourish. This is because parents are permitted to set up the kind of school they desire for their children and many prefer small schools. The state provides support to private schools to the extent of 85% of the running costs. This allows for considerable variety and choice, as the legal requirements that have to be met when a new small school starts are not insurmountable. The school must have a minimum of twelve students during the first year of operation, twenty in the second year and a minimum of twenty seven thereafter. The average size of the schools is sixty and the range is between thirty and one hundred. The supervision of the school is left almost entirely to the parents and they appoint a suitable person to monitor basic attainment standards. As a result there is considerable variety in the philosophies of education represented in different schools. One group identified by de la Cour, for example, about forty five schools, are parent-teacher co-operative small schools that have come out of the alternative movements of the late 1960s and which are known as 'humanistic' schools. As de la Cour notes, the Danish system is extremely facilitative and positively encourages educational diversity, choice and innovation.

Running Small Schools Effectively

Most governments now accept the need for small schools and their importance as part of their overall educational provision. However, small schools can face particular problems and issues and a number of publications (Bray 1987a, Hopkins and Ellis 1991 and Department for Education 1993) have suggested a series of principles for maximising the effectiveness of small schools, some of which are summarised below.

Finance:

- Small schools may have higher unit costs than large schools. Governments and local authorities should recognise this if it is the case and give them favourable treatment in financial allocations.
- If such support is insufficient it can be offset to some extent by good relationships with the community.

Teaching and Learning:

- Teachers need to ensure their teaching methods are appropriate and relevant. In mixed age range classes teaching approaches need to be flexible and based largely on individual and small group activities rather than on class lessons.
- Teachers therefore need to be reflective and should continually re-examine and evaluate their teaching strategies.
- The school should therefore have a well considered policy on mixed age range teaching.

Staffing:

- During pre-service teacher training courses, examine methods for multi-grade work. If teaching practice cannot be arranged in ordinary small schools, set up special model ones.
- Stress the professional rewards of work in small schools and try to attract teachers who will take it as a worthwhile challenge.
- Provide a reasonable career structure. Avoid the situation in which teachers get promotion only in large schools.
- Give teachers professional support in the form of in-service courses for staff who have been in small schools for several years

and who need to reflect on methods; opportunities to visit other small schools and to exchange ideas; advisory visits by advisers and inspectors; support for associations of teachers in small schools.
- Train all teachers in an least two subject areas.
- Examine the potential for mobile teachers and sharing of staff resources.

Materials and Facilities:

- Devote resources to curriculum development, e.g. special textbooks and self-instructional materials for multi-grade classes.
- Build large classrooms and provide furniture that is easily moved when group work in multi-grade classes is needed.
- Encourage schools that are reasonably close to each other to share equipment and resources (school clustering is discussed in more detail on the next section of this book).
- Provide school broadcasts and bear the needs of small schools in mind during preparation.
- Establish correspondence courses and make them available to students in small schools.

Community Involvement:

- Recognise that communities are particularly likely to display a strong interest in the activities of small schools. Make sure that teachers are sensitive to the positive and negative aspects of this.
- Explore ways of to use parents and other community members in terms of auxiliary teaching, fund raising and administration.

Conclusion

The arguments used against small schools do not seem to be supported by the evidence and there are good reasons why this is the case. In terms of school effectiveness, however understood and measured, small schools seem to have some major advantages both socially and educationally. This is particularly so in relation to the potential social costs of large schools. Small schools are not without their potential problems, however, and have to be carefully managed both internally and by the state. The next section of the book examines how some of these problems can be mitigated or removed by co-operation between small schools and by decentralising large schools.

Chapter two

Making Large Schools Smaller and Small Schools Larger

Introduction

The potential problems of small schools are, for example, isolation and less adequate fixed resources such as libraries and science facilities. Is it possible to have some of the best of both? This section examines two possibilities, the idea that existing large schools can become 'smaller' through reorganisation into smaller units (mini-schooling) and the practice of school clustering where a number of smaller schools co-operate with each other to improve the education in each.

Minischooling

Ernest L. Bayer, the influential President of the Carnegie Foundation for the Advancement of Teaching, addressed President Bush with these words:

> *"If I had one wish for school reform I would break up every...school into units of no more than 400 students each."*
> *(quoted in Anderson, 1991:14).*

Indeed, as a result of continual school violence, a high school in New York was closed and replaced by the 'Urban Academy' consisting of four small high schools with a maximum of 300 students each, an elementary school, a teen parenting resources centre, a professional development centre, a transitional college programme and comprehensive medical services. According to the National Centre for Restructuring Education, which monitors new initiatives in high schooling, the success of the Urban Academy,

"Illustrates the consistent findings of recent research showing that smaller schools that are organised to provide continuous relationships among adults and young people and that focus on meaningful and challenging kinds of learning are more successful at motivating, engaging and graduating students and ensuring their later success." (quoted in Hodgetts 1995).

'Mini-schooling' is a method of organising a large school into small sub-units that has been used in Britain. Each sub-unit or mini-school has its own small team of teachers, its own population of students, its own area or base in the school, some autonomy over its use of time and some resources of its own. The best documented example of this is Madeley Court, a large secondary school in Shropshire where the head teacher, Philip Toogood, organised the first three years of the school along the lines of six mini-schools of 100 students each, between 1977 and 1983 (see, for example, Toogood 1992). The aim of this structure was to give teachers and learners effective power and control over their daily learning, supported and monitored by a central 'federal' team.

The use of space in a school says a great deal about its aims and ideology. Despite his use of gendered language the American educationalist Herbert Kohl captured this well when he argued that,

"The placement of objects in space is not arbitrary and rooms represent in physical form the spirit and souls of places and institutions. A teacher's room tells us something about who he is and a great deal about what he is doing." (Kohl 1970).

Most secondary schools are organised spatially in terms of subjects areas with students wandering from one area to another during the day with no space of their own. The basis of the mini-schools at Madeley Court, however, was territorial. Each of the six mini-school populations with their four core teachers of maths, science, English and social science, and their two attached tutors from out-base subjects, together with the parents, 'owned' a territory of their own, usually referred to as 'the base'. It was , with rare exceptions, used only by them and was maintained to a high standard of both fabric and display. Teachers, parents and students would often make up working parties to transform the mini-school by painting and other minor improvements.

Each base had four linked, open-plan areas, a small science lab, a parent-teacher office and toilets in it or near it. Bases were usually accessible by a staircase and were not a thoroughfare so that others could get 'to' somewhere else. The mini-school team was in the base from 8.30 in the morning until the end of after-school activities. Toogood argues that the bases were the learning homes within the school - not just the pastoral base but the whole learning home for the sharing of the daily activities. He comments that,

> "I used to imagine what image the child had in mind as he or she walked into school. Certainly they saw a small school, personal to them with all the plants, experiments, the mini-school microcomputers, the walls decorated by them, the inviolable displays of their own work and their own tutor base in one of the four areas. This was an important element in building up that sense of belonging and of motivation to go to school without which discipline and co-operation are so lacking." (1992:29).

Toogood argues that this form of spatial ownership had a number of significant advantages:

(i) Parents would regularly come into concerts, drama, beetle drives, jumble sales, wine and cheese parties, subject evenings, report evenings and PTA mini-school committee meetings because the bases were on a scale that they were places to remember and care about.

(ii) The need for bells and corridor circulation disappears and the school became a much quieter learning place.

(iii) Theft in the mini-schools was almost totally absent.

(iv) Attendance was well over 90% on average.

(v) Learning spaces and timetables were flexible and could be arranged rapidly to suit diverse learning requirements.

(vi) Parents, teachers and students felt passionately about 'their' mini-school. In 1982 the schools raised 30,000 pounds sterling towards the students' education - more than the annual per capita allowance from the local education authority.

(vii) The flexible learning environment allowed the accommodation of students with special educational needs that would otherwise have had to have gone to a special school.

(viii) The teachers related to each other as people and not members of a subject specialist team, though each teacher had a subject responsibility and was linked to the subject team for discussion, resources and support. However, the teachers learnt more about relating to children in this environment than in the traditional specialist area base.

Toogood notes that while schools adapt quite easily to the structure of territory for mini-schools, the main problem is maintaining focal points for subject specialisms, However, he sees this as more of a problem of how to construct an adequate resource centre than of actually constructing areas where all the teaching and learning in a subject can be done. Another issue was of maintaining some central co-ordination. There were regular meetings of heads every half year, including the mini-school heads, and the heads of department. Also important was the establishment of small ad hoc working parties which could be set up by anyone - the central team, mini-school team, pastoral or academic group or even an individual teacher. The working party had to register the activity with the central team (head and deputies) and the findings had to be reported on a timed schedule to a staff meeting - the central team might receive the document first or after discussion in a wider staff forum.

Another school that has adopted the mini-schooling model is Stantonbury Campus, a secondary school of over 2,000 students in Milton Keynes, UK. Its aim is to combine the variety of resource provision that size can bring without becoming impersonal. The prospectus notes that the school,

"...combines the flexibility and richness of resources that size brings with an organisation that allows each student to feel secure and special, and that encourages individual challenge" (quoted in Meighan, 1995:47).

Stantonbury calls its sub-units 'halls'. The school is divided into five halls - one for post-16 year olds and the other four operate as mini-schools, each composed of about 450 students working with 30 staff members. Students are encouraged through a scheme of campus service to participate in the wider life of the campus and to gain experience of working in the community.

School Clusters

Bray (1987b:7) defines a school cluster as 'a grouping of schools for administrative and educational purposes'. The idea is that small schools, while retaining their advantages as human scale organisations serving a particular community, can also benefit through co-operation with each other. There is considerable variety in the different possible models for operating a school cluster. The model adopted will depend partly on the number of schools involved (these can vary from four to forty) and the main purposes of the particular cluster. Bray (1987b) provides a useful categorisation of such purposes according to economic, pedagogic, administrative and political objectives from which the following discussion is adapted.

Economic

Sharing of facilities: these can include equipment such as sports, science, musical, computer and agricultural equipment; textbooks and library books and buildings such as science laboratories, sports buildings and theatres.

Sharing staff: these can be either specialist staff such as language or music teachers or non-teaching staff such as typists or accountants. Such staff can either spend part of the week in each school or be assigned to individual schools for periods of time. Cluster systems also provide pools of teachers who can be used in emergencies so that if a teacher in a single or two teacher school is absent then children do not have to be sent home, because a

teacher can be transferred from another school until the original
teacher returns.

Bulk ordering of materials: if schools group together they can
usually get discounts from suppliers through bulk ordering.
Moreover, some suppliers may only be willing to meet orders
above a certain size, which can disadvantage small schools.

Pedagogic

Teacher development: teachers in small schools can run the risk
of becoming isolated and inward-looking. Cluster meetings can
help teachers to share ideas and experience and to tackle problems
jointly.

Curriculum development: clusters can also be used to hold
workshops on new syllabuses, teaching materials and methods.

School Projects: cluster schools can join together for educational
visits. This may decrease the cost of transport to and entry into,
for example, museums and historical sites.
It also increases the number of peers with which the students
interact.

Inter-school events: These can be, for example, sports fixtures,
debating societies and musical and theatrical events.

Linkages between levels and types of education: some school
clusters deliberately link together primary and secondary schools
in order that primary schools can gain access to the (usually more
plentiful) facilities of the secondary schools; so that primary
schools can gain access to the (usually more highly qualified) staff
of the secondary schools and so that secondary schools can gain
better understanding of the backgrounds from which the students
come to them. Some cluster schemes in Sri Lanka, Ecuador and
Peru have aimed to link schools with non-formal education. The
latter has particularly benefited from the resources and the
institutional frameworks of the schools.

Administrative

From the point of view of the local authority: clusters can mean that local or district levels of education have to deal with fewer individuals. Information can be sent to the cluster co-ordinator rather than to individual schools. School statistics can be collected by the cluster co-ordinator before being sent on to the local authority. Cluster co-ordinators become an obvious choice to represent their clusters at planning meetings, thereby facilitating consultation without necessitating too many separate meetings.

From the point of view of the cluster: there is strength in numbers. Operating as a cluster of a number of schools means that viewpoints and requests are more likely to be listened to by local government than if they came from individual schools. The case study from Namibia described below illustrates this point.

Political

Bray (1987b) describes how school clusters have been used for political objectives in some developing countries.

Community participation: several schemes in India have tried to use school clusters to revitalise parent-teacher associations.

Reduced inequalities: cluster schemes can attempt to reduce inequalities by encouraging well-endowed, prosperous schools to share their resources with less fortunate ones.

Ethnic and/or religious harmony: in Sri Lanka school clusters were specifically designed to promote ethnic harmony. Clusters deliberately grouped together the schools of different ethnic groups in order to encourage communication and a framework of common activities. This seems an idea applicable to any society where groups that have traditionally been hostile to each other live in close proximity. Examples would be clashes of religion/national identity in Northern Ireland, language differences in Belgium or Canada, or 'racial' differences in South Africa.

Case Studies of School Clusters

The following are accounts of how actual school clusters have operated. They are drawn from a range of countries and exhibit many of the objectives outlined above. However, it is important to bear in mind that, although each case study concerns clusters, the social, economic, political and educational contexts in which the various clusters operate are very different from each other and therefore the needs and priorities of the schools concerned will also vary considerably. This is an important point as, although there may be some common themes, what makes a small school or a school cluster 'effective' (or 'ineffective') will differ according to context (see Harber 1992). (Educational management in the context of developing countries in particular, is further discussed in Harber (1993a) and Davies and Harber, forthcoming.)

Namibia

This case study, with which the writer was personally involved, was established as a result of the Nuffield Foundation funding four Namibian head teachers to visit the UK for a term at the end of 1993. The four head teachers were all from small, rural primary schools in northern Namibia. Three of the four were also very isolated - one, for example, being 40 kilometres from the tarmac road. On returning to Namibia in late 1993 the head teachers each decided that they would try to establish a cluster based on their own schools. When the writer visited the four head teachers in August 1994 these had been established and ranged from 7 to 10 schools in each cluster. Some of the issues that the clusters has discussed or acted upon included the following:

(a) The problem of school admissions given that there are too many children for too few seats.

(b) The problem of maintaining educational motivation - in one cluster a 'motivation meeting' was held at one of the schools which was attended by teachers, parents, inspectors and over 300 students.

(c) The problem of teaching materials and methods - ideas and resources have been exchanged, e.g. in relation to mathematics education.

(d) The problem of under-staffing and under-qualified staff. One cluster persuaded the Ministry to transfer 13 of the 49 teachers at the local secondary school, which was over-staffed in terms of staff-student ratios, to their primary schools. The Nuffield head teacher himself received two extra qualified teachers. If one head teacher had asked for such transfers it is very likely that nothing would have happened but when ten schools raise the issue together they are listened to and stand a better chance of achieving their aims. Similarly, the cluster asked for new buildings and the Nuffield head teacher received a new classroom which he had needed for some years.

(e) Each of the schools in one cluster contributed 20 Namibian dollars so that they could purchase a duplicating machine. This runs off electricity and so is based at the local secondary school which has electricity. Each primary school in the cluster can go to the secondary school and use the machine when they want to. (It is worth noting that the possession of a duplicating machine is not a trivial matter to schools in developing countries. Vulliamy (1987) in his research in rural Papua New Guinea, found that the possession of a duplicating machine made a significant difference to a school's effectiveness. This is because, in the absence of other forms of reprographic machinery, the possession of a duplicating machine permitting the production of quantities of worksheets greatly facilitates a broader range of teaching methods than simply chalk and talk.

(f) Meetings were held in one cluster to discuss management styles, as some heads have found it difficult to move from traditional, authoritarian management to the new official emphasis on participation, co-operation and teamwork.

(g) The success of clusters is also helped if extra money can be raised for joint projects. At one of the Nuffield head teacher's schools they started a bakery to get funds for the cluster while at another they had raised nearly 2,000 dollars for the cluster.

Britain
One of the areas that the Nuffield Fellows visited in Britain in order to see school clusters in operation was Wales. Recent research on school clusters in Wales (Potter and Williams, 1994)

looked at two clusters each of five schools, though one was in a rural area and one in an urban area. Three head teachers from each cluster were interviewed. The head teachers were asked what they perceived to be the most important advantage that they had gained from clustering. In the rural cluster two of the three head teachers identified opportunities for pupils to meet each other socially as the most important aspect of clustering and the third head teacher, although not putting this first, agreed that it was very important. She said,

> *"The more opportunity they have to meet other children the more confident they become. They need new relationships as many of these children are not only isolated in schools but lots of them are isolated on their farms. The school is the only time they meet friends and many would never go a mile or two down the road." (p.149)*

The cluster had organised a sports day with all of the students in each of the five rural schools being assigned to mixed teams so that the students interacted with others all day without inter-school rivalry. Other social events included attendance at a performance by a visiting theatre group, joint residential visits to an outdoor pursuits centre and an annual trip either to London or the Isle of Wight. The third head teacher chose 'less professional isolation for teachers' as her major benefit, asserting that,

> *"In rural areas like this, you can be very isolated so that clustering is the saviour of small schools. It opens many avenues for the teachers to get together and share their expertise and feeling that they are doing the right thing. It builds up confidence - it takes time but it breaks down lots of barriers." (p.149)*

In the town cluster all three head teachers saw clustering as a means of lessening professional isolation but they also stressed that the cluster had become a mechanism for getting extra resources from the local authority.

Another recent study of the Ashby cluster in the east of Northamptonshire (Atkins and Rivers, 1994) argued that,

"In spite of the additional layer which clustering brings to the workload of all concerned, there is a strong feeling within the cluster that the positive ethos is essential to the continuing development of education in small schools." *(p.16)*

The article on the school cluster analysed the benefits of the cluster in terms of what was in it for the different groups concerned:

Children: the limited peer groups in small schools are extended in such activities as residential and other visits, peer group curricular and other curricular activities, curriculum workshops aimed at particular ages and stages and linked project work. Peer groups across the schools are well developed before secondary education begins, thus minimising the problem of small school secondary transfer.

Teaching staff: The 20 full-time teaching staff in the Ashby cluster have been planning the curriculum together and working consecutively on whole school modules which have been planned in teams of three across the cluster. This has led to a vastly reduced workload for all teachers and has added the strength of teamwork consolidated by the sharing of professional development days. Promotion prospects, which do not necessarily abound in small schools, are available to staff interested in becoming cluster co-ordinators in the core and foundation subjects of the national curriculum. The responsibility of the co-ordinators includes leading the rest of the cluster staff in the formation of cluster policy in their subject which is a good opportunity for personal development not normally available in small schools. Several support groups have been formed, such as the Early Years group in which the staff have worked through their own development planning process to identify beneficial issues and have worked on a shared induction programme plan.

Head teachers:
The head teachers have gained by the sharing of the management load facilitated by the close network of shared responsibilities designated in the cluster development plan. The heads have

regular management meetings where actions and responsibilities are agreed with agendas set as a group. It is also stimulating to individual school heads to have the opportunity to extend their own personal professional development through contact with other heads and other teaching staff.

Support staff:
The support staff have set up their own network of help and advice in the light of government reforms such as the decentralisation of budgets under the local management of schools.

Parents:
Through the peer group activities and residentials, their children are more confident about approaching secondary transfer. The secondary school fed by the cluster talks to the cluster parents together, in a cluster venue, to endorse this link. Such activities as games, which are difficult in small schools, are extended by after-school cluster clubs, fully supported by parents with an interest in those fields.

Governors:
Through the cluster Governors' Steering Committee, opportunities are provided for governors to identify and receive training as a cluster in regard to such areas as pay policy and special needs. The governors also feel that they have the strength of speaking as a cluster if the need arises.

India
Bray (1987b:72) reports an interesting case study from Maharashtra State in India. Charholi Complex was launched in 1977 and has one high school (which has been made the central school), two elementary schools and six primary schools. One of the primary schools has only one teacher and two have two teachers. None of the schools is more than six kilometres from the central school.

Every year the complex committee grades each member school on its environment, management, educational progress, supervision and links with the community. The grading helps diagnose problems and assess progress. The scale has five points (A-E). In

1977, three schools scored D and six scored E. But by 1981 four schools scored B, four scored C and one scored D. This reflected improvements caused by the complex activities. Particularly notable achievements were:

- increase in the Grade 1 enrolment rate from 85% to 100%.
- reduction in the Grade 1 drop out rate from 56% in 1976 to 12% in 1980.
- reduction in repetition from about 400 students a year to about 100 students a year.
- improvement in the pass rate in the school certificate examination from 21% in 1976 to 67% in 1980.
- marked improvements in buildings, school gardens and other facilities.

One instrument for improvement has been a teacher self-evaluation project organised by the complex. In addition the organisation of school projects has effectively mobilised community support. Whereas in 1975 only Rs.219 were contributed by communities, in 1980 contributions reached Rs.1,401 and in 1981 - a year of particularly notable activity - Rs.542,002.

Bray, however, notes that the Charholi complex cannot be taken as typical as it has been personally supervised by the Director of Education and has been designated a model for the state. He argues that it nevertheless indicates the extent to which the complex idea can promote improvements. Indeed, most of the examples used so far illustrate the benefits of clustering. However, as the final case study from Thailand suggests, while clustering has many potential benefits, these are not always easy to achieve, especially if the cluster was not voluntary in the first place. It also shows that there can be considerable variation in approach and emphasis both between clusters and between the individual schools that go to make up the cluster.

Thailand
In 1980 the previously voluntary cluster arrangement for primary schools in Thailand became compulsory. By the late 1980s they were aimed at pursuing two approaches to primary school

improvement.   First, a capacity-building approach which emphasises staff development, local improvement initiatives and intrinsic rewards such as a professional commitment to teaching and, second, an accountability approach emphasising rules and regulations, testing and extrinsic rewards such as promotions.

Tsang and Wheeler (1993) studied two clusters in one area of Thailand. In one cluster, testing formed the cornerstone of the cluster's accountability approach to school improvement, an approach that dominated more limited efforts towards capacity building such as staff development. In response to a national focus on improving test scores the cluster set up a working group to develop cluster tests for various grades in the schools. To motivate teachers to improve through competition, the cluster office tabulates the results and publishes them by school and by grade so that every teacher knows where he or she stands compared to other teachers in the cluster. Principals are encouraged to use test results as one criterion for teacher evaluation purposes in recommending promotions. Classroom teachers are not involved in the construction of any tests; the working group develops all the items for the cluster test and submits suggested items to the district office for its tests. Because of the emphasis on improving test scores, teachers across the schools in the cluster report a decline in interest in spending time on   school-wide   activities   or   volunteering   for.   cluster responsibilities because these detract from the time available to teach in their own classrooms.

The effects of this emphasis on testing, however, varied from one school to another. In one school the principal used the test results as a justification for changing the reward system from a rotation system whereby a different teacher each year was given an extra promotion regardless of student performance, to a merit system where student performance became one of several important criteria for an extra promotion. In another school the principal used the test results as a rationale for convincing parents to purchase supplementary textbooks (the next year the school moved from sixth to second within the cluster). Two other principals used the test results as explicit justifications for their decisions several years earlier to move to a merit system of recommending extra promotions.   Principals in three other schools simply ignored the test results, as did most of the teachers in these schools.

In contrast to the first cluster, the second cluster showed that the cluster has the capacity to pursue effectively both the capacity-building and the accountability approaches. In terms of capacity-building, staff in this cluster took advantage of every opportunity to host staff development initiatives from the national, provincial and district offices. The teachers, in contrast to most of their counterparts in the other cluster, were active in assisting colleagues in their respective schools to improve their pedagogy. The working group in this cluster was also more active in developing materials and in involving teachers from individual schools in materials development after schools hours and on Saturdays. Such activities also affected what teachers did in the classrooms. The researchers observed a greater variety of teaching styles and use of teaching materials in the schools in this cluster.

However, as with the first cluster, the schools varied in their response to the level of cluster activity. One principal went so far as to close the entire school whenever the cluster was sponsoring staff development activities so that all staff could participate and substituting school days at the weekend (with staff support) so that students would not miss out on teaching time. A principal in another school was far less supportive and made no special arrangements to facilitate staff involvement; not surprisingly, a smaller percentage of the staff participated in these activities.

Conclusion

This section has suggested that large schools do not necessarily have to be a barrier to human scale education. Through reorganisation into mini-schools some of the benefits of scale can be retained while reducing the disadvantages of impersonality and alienation associated with large schools. Conversely, small schools can retain their identity and independence while co-operating in clusters with other small schools to bring about benefits for them all. As the above discussion has also suggested, there is no single model for a school cluster, as school clustering is a widespread international phenomenon and can exist for a diverse range of reasons and purposes, even within the same country. One such purpose can be the education of democratic citizens, though this is not an aim regularly made explicit in the literature either on small schools or on school clusters. Moreover, neither of the two case studies of mini-schooling have operated as democratic schools. The final section of the book looks at the potential for small schools to operate as democratic institutions.

Chapter three

Small Schools and Democratic Education

Introduction

Since the collapse of communism at the end of the 1980s there has been a renewed interest in democracy world-wide. Many formerly authoritarian one-party or military regimes in areas such as South America, eastern Europe, Africa and Asia have held multi-party elections. At the same time western support for democracy in these regions has led to debates in some western countries themselves about how democratic their political institutions and societies really are. An example of this is the Charter 88 pressure group in Britain which promotes a set of proposals significantly to increase the democratic nature of political institutions in Britain. A sub-theme of the debates on democratisation has been a debate on the role played by education in sustaining democracy in the longer run. If democracy can survive only in a society that possesses democratic values, and given that such values are socially learned and not genetic, what role can small schools play in developing democratic values?

Schools and Values

> *"Children who are lectured, learn how to lecture; if they are admonished, they learn how to admonish; if scolded they learn how to scold; if ridiculed, they learn how to ridicule; if humiliated they learn how to humiliate; if their psyche is killed, they will learn how to kill - the only question is who will be killed: oneself, others or both?"* (Alice Miller, quoted in Meighan, 1994:69).

It has long been recognised that schools play a significant part in the learning of values and behaviours and that, as the above quotation suggests, this has as much if not more to do with how schools and classrooms are organised than what is taught. I have argued elsewhere (Harber 1995: chapter 1) that research internationally from areas as geographically and politically diverse as Canada, the USA, Africa, China, Latin America, Cuba and the UK indicates that schooling is overwhelmingly an authoritarian experience for students. Students have little say in how the school is organised, the decisions that are made on their behalf, and what is taught and how. School is a hierarchical experience and learning is largely a passive process of absorbing information selected by others.

Unfortunately, despite their potential for very different relationships, many small schools would currently fall into the authoritarian category, albeit that it is often a benevolent and well-meaning form of authoritarianism. In arguing in favour of small schools, for example, Philip Toogood nevertheless notes that,

> "I learnt that it is possible to be small and ugly. Smallness does not in itself guarantee democratic practice and creative learning. In fact, when you get autocratic practice in a small institution you can have the worst of all worlds because there is no escape for the victim, the student. At this point the inefficiency and crass stupidity of the mass system seems like heaven." (1991:4).

The enhanced quality and closer nature of student-teacher relationships that are possible in small schools mean that they have the potential to develop as democratic institutions more readily than larger schools. However, while small schools have the potential to operate as democratic institutions, there is nothing in the size of a school which makes it inherently or inevitably democratic. The following describes a school of 30 students in rural Natal, South Africa in the 1850s,

> "Punishment was brutal. On the least provocation a boy would get a clout on the head, politely termed a "box on the ears". For offences which Brown (the head teacher) felt deserved a flogging, the oak tree still growing at the entrance to the churchyard provided the saplings.

Thrashings were of daily occurrence and inflicted for quite trivial offences, as the following illustration will make evident. Every morning we were lined up, and made to take our turn in reading aloud. Alan Moodie was unfortunate enough to possess a stammer. He dreaded having to encounter in the course of his passage the word "but". Brown used to tell him to take a deep breath to help him over the dreaded word. This only seemed to make the boy more nervous. One day he broke down altogether. Brown had no sympathy for him. The sapling was produced, and Moodie, his trousers pulled down below his knees, was hustled across a desk. Brown caned him for stupidity and defiance until the cane drew blood. He then ordered the rest of us to send him to Coventry for the rest of the week." (Hattersley, 1936:229).

Yet if schools do help to shape the values of children, then to reproduce authoritarian modes of thought and behaviour is at best not helpful to democracy and is at worst dangerous to it. In order to promote and sustain democratic values there must be a conscious, explicit and continual effort at political education in such democratic values as tolerance of diversity, mutual respect, equal human rights, political choice and freedom of thought. For schools to neglect them simply leaves in place a status quo which in many countries is not necessarily or wholly supportive of democracy. This is certainly recognised in the former communist countries of eastern Europe. Dneprov (1995), for example, the Minister of Education for the Russian Federation from 1989-1992, talks of the need to use education to help to change the mentality of society, to change the system of values away from totalitarianism and to promote democratic decision-making and independence. Ironically, as Brown (1995) points out, because of the history of the last 50 years, educators in eastern Europe are far more aware of this than educators in the west. He notes, for example, how teachers in Lithuania had some difficulty grasping that schools in Britain display few of the democratic characteristics that they are trying to introduce into Lithuania. Thorpe (1994) makes the same point in relation to Russia.

Indeed, Britain is a disturbing case study of the neglect of political education for democracy. An important aspect of this, for example, is racism. Racism is a worrying part of British society and schools have often either reproduced it by ignoring it or actually contributed to it through teacher attitudes, educational employment policies and the content of curriculum and textbooks (Harber 1990). The outcome of this is endemic political ignorance and racism among white youth in Britain. A summary of six research projects carried out by the Economic and Social Research Council in the early and mid-1980s on 16-19 year olds (McGurk, 1987) found not only that this was the case but that many young people conceded that with greater knowledge they would not have reached racist conclusions and expressed regret that they had not had more political education in school. McGurk concluded that,

> *"Lacking any political education in the broadest sense, young people will continue to exist in a condition of ignorance in which simple solutions, especially racist ones, will have appeal. This is not necessarily because of their intrinsic attractiveness, but because of a lack of perceived alternatives. Some of the respondents in the present study seemed aware of this danger and wanted the sort of information that prevents them from being drawn into racist simplicities. The policy implications are clear. The current reluctance to introduce political studies into the school curriculum needs to be re-evaluated." (1987:51).*

Ironically, this statement was made at the very moment the British government was introducing a national curriculum which deliberately excluded the subject. Indeed, a further major study of 16-19 year olds published since the introduction of a national curriculum is also highly critical of its failure in regard to political education,

> *"Perhaps the most disturbing aspect of our findings was the political apathy and the incoherence of much of the political opinion that our respondents expressed. Concentrated among early school leavers, this is to be seen as another form of inequality. Again, those proceeding with education have a sense of political efficacy which goes on strengthening as they stay on. Those who leave for the ostensibly adult world of the workplace are not only the most politically alienated but are also likely to be the most*

impotent. Clearly, for a democracy to have meaning, it must be accessible to and understood by all its citizens. Even the act of voting was rejected by up to 15% of our 18 year olds. It seems that the pre-16 school curriculum and education policy generally have been neglectful in this respect. Educational institutions offer numerous opportunities for enabling young people to gain understanding of and to exercise political responsibility at the classroom, school and community level. The curriculum, too, can be made more relevant and meaningful to young people by creating space in it for them to engage continually with current events. Most other European countries recognise the importance of such education for citizenship. The national curriculum in England and Wales needs to recognise it too." (Banks et al, 1992:187).

Democratic Education

The need for political education for democracy is indeed recognised in Europe. The appendix to Recommendation R(85) of the committee of ministers of the Council of Europe to member states on teaching and learning about human rights in schools notes the importance of school atmosphere or ethos in educating for democracy,

"Democracy is best learned in a democratic setting where participation is encouraged, where views are can be expressed openly and discussed, where there is freedom of expression for pupils and teachers, and where there is fairness and justice. An appropriate climate is, therefore, an essential complement to effective teaching and learning about human rights." (Starkey, 1991:222).

A democratic school is one where the power of decision-making is shared between the major groups involved in the school - teachers, students and parents. There is no single, clear-cut organisational model of a democratic school. Indeed, if the participants are to shape the way a school is organised there can be no clear and precise blueprint. However, the following list of key characteristics is compiled from descriptions of those few schools which have operated democratically in Britain and in other European countries such as Denmark, Holland, France and Germany (Harber and Meighan, 1989; Jensen and Walker 1989). As the list suggests, the formal structures, principles and processes of such schools typically embody notions of power-sharing, representation, co-operation, openness and participation:

- students have influence over what is taught and learned
- the shared part of the curriculum embodies some analysis of contemporary society
- students, staff and parents are all part of the school's decision-making process, usually through some form of school council
- representation on decision-making bodies is by election
- school councils meet during school time
- teaching method is participatory and active as well as teacher-led
- staff (and in some cases students) are involved in the selection of new staff
- parents are regarded as partners with open access
- physical punishment is absent
- an informal, relaxed and friendly atmosphere with use of first names, no separate staff or dining rooms and no uniform
- students have a right to freedom of expression.

To this list would now have to be added the existence of an active equal opportunities or equal rights policy to combat any discrimination in school practices on the grounds of 'race', gender or disability.

Democratic education is by no means confined to secondary education. However, while in primary schools classroom teaching and learning is often more child-centred and active, school councils that play a significant role in the school life are less common. One study of 123 primary schools in Canada, for example, found that where schools had councils (56 out of 123) they were in practice only given a very limited role, confined to fund raising and planning social events. Yet in the two schools where genuine provision was made for student council input on school issues, students and staff alike agreed that the student council input was invaluable in the solution of school problems. The authors commented that,

"The failure of administrators and teachers to give students more opportunities for input into the running of schools represents a great loss to education. Numerous studies have pointed to the substantial benefits that accrue to both students and schools when there are effectively functioning student councils in schools. What is perhaps even more important is that students' basic attitudes towards politics are shaped by students' participation in school governance." (Robinson and Koehn, 1994:26).

Harber (1995: chapter 2) provides examples of the operation of such councils in primary schools.

Moreover, research evidence suggests that a democratic school environment can indeed foster democratic values, skills and behaviours. Hepburn, summarising five pieces of research in the United States, concluded that,

"Collectively, the five research studies reviewed here provide evidence that democratic schooling is more than just a philosopher's dream. Carried out in different conceptual frameworks with differing methods, these studies indicate that democratic education is not only possible but that it is feasible, even within the bureaucratic structure of American schools and in the shifting attitudes of society. Moreover, the five studies add to the evidence, collected in other democratic countries, that democratic experiences in the school and the classroom do contribute to the participatory awareness, skills and attitudes fundamental to life in democratic societies." (1984:261).

Research in Britain, (John and Osborn 1992) compared two secondary schools, one traditional and authoritarian and one democratic in terms of the development of civic attitudes. The research suggested that there were somewhat stronger democratic attitudes among the students from the democratic school than the traditional one. Also, students at the democratic school were more ardent supporters of race and gender equality, but were more sceptical about whether the government actually operated democratically. The findings also suggested that the democratic school was also more likely to encourage freedom of expression in the classroom.

In interviews carried out by the writer in two schools in Tanzania with active school councils, it was noted by both staff and students that they felt that participation, apart from improving certain aspects of school management, had helped to develop responsibility, confidence, problem-solving through discussion and a friendlier and more co-operative environment (Harber 1993b). In 1976, during the Eritrean war of independence against Ethiopia, the Eritrean Peoples Liberation Front opened what became known as the 'Zero School' to provide education for young Eritreans who had fled from the Ethiopian occupation. Both the school structures and informal relationships were democratic. As the director of the school concluded,

> "Therefore, the Zero School tried to make decisions collectively and encouraged students to participate actively and trained them to be good citizens who were free to give suggestions and opinions...students were responsible and disciplined and their academic achievement was high but beyond this they were tolerant and critical." (Tesfamariam, 1993:14).

After the war some 500 students from the school were moved to a new site at Decamare some 40 kilometres from the capital, Asmara. Here they attend a local school but live in dormitories in what was until 1991 an Ethiopian army base. The writer visited the school in early 1995 and found that the ethos of the Zero School had had a strong impact on the students. The dormitories are ethnically mixed, and there is a strongly co-operative and friendly atmosphere. There is a council composed of elected representatives from the dormitories which meets once a month but can meet weekly if issues arise. The students expressed their concerns about the problems of integrating into the local, 'normal' school. They said that they were used to teachers who treated them as equals and discussed in a participatory manner. They pointed out that, whereas teachers in the Zero School would encourage questions, even if they were not particularly good ones, the teachers in the present school discouraged questions and even scolded them if they asked. The trust and equality they were used to were not present in the school but they were determined to maintain it in the dormitories.

Similar problems of reintegration have been faced by Namibian students who attended the SWAPO (South West Africa Peoples Organisation) school at Loudima in Congo Brazzaville. After independence the students from Loudima were moved to a 'normal' school at Mweshipandeka in northern Namibia. The students from Loudima who were used to a learner-centred curriculum that used group work, discussion and critical thinking and which encouraged them to challenge teachers, were seen as rude and lacking respect by existing students and some of the teachers (Brock-Utne, Appiah-Endresen and Oliver, 1994:17).

There is also evidence that more open, democratic classrooms can foster a range of democratic political orientations such as greater political interest, less authoritarianism, greater political knowledge and a greater sense of political efficacy (Ehman, 1980). Democratic and co-operative teaching methods have also been shown to reduce inter-ethnic conflict and to promote cross-cultural conflict (Lynch, 1991:22). A study of ethnically mixed schools in the south eastern United States compared two schools that stressed co-operative learning, the development of interpersonal relationships, values clarification and the heterogeneous grouping of students, with three traditional schools where students were streamed by achievement and taught in a lecture-recitation style in predominantly same-'race' classes. The study found that cross-'race' interaction and friendships and a positive evaluation of different 'race' students were significantly higher in the former than in the latter (Conway and Damico 1993).

Moreover, a recent review of the school effectiveness literature, while correctly noting the problematic nature of judging school effectiveness, nevertheless concluded that many of the structures and processes which characterise effective schools in meeting the learning needs of their students, align with democratic principles and practice. Effective leadership is seen in terms of empowering others rather than exercising power over others. In terms of classroom management, classroom organisation which encourages and rewards student involvement is linked to higher learning.

Achievement is higher where students take responsibility for their own learning. Effective schools are those which encourage a mix of teaching and learning methods that includes individualised and co-operative learning as well as limited amounts of enthusiastic and motivated whole class teaching. In terms of student care, students in effective schools are treated with dignity and encouraged to participate in the organisation of the school, including the primary school, and as a result they feel valued. The effective school culture includes many of the core values associated with democracy, such as tolerating and respecting others, participating and expressing views, sharing and disseminating knowledge, valuing equity and equality and the opportunity for students to make judgements and choices (Dimmock, 1995:163-7).

An example of where a democratic approach has helped to make schools more effective comes from the state of Victoria, Australia:

> *"Democratic approaches have allowed the introduction of such qualities as innovation, participation, co-operation, autonomy, individualisation and initiative in both staff and pupils as characterising the ethos of a successful comprehensive school, for it is these qualities which can support the democratic principles of tolerance and equity between human beings" (quoted in Dunstan, 1995:121).*

Democracy in Small Schools

At a conference of democratic schools attended by the writer and held at Sands School in Devon at the end of March 1994, what was immediately noticeable was the small size of the schools involved. Sands itself has 30 students, Park School has 65 students, Summerhill 65 students, Willington 14 students, Hartland 30 students and Freie Gesamtschule in Austria 12 students. Sudbury Valley School in the USA, which could not attend as its representatives were at another conference, has about 90-100 students. The largest school was Hadera School from Israel with 300 students. This is undoubtedly because it is a state school and under pressures that private schools are not. Even keeping the numbers down to 300 has not been easy - it already has 2,500 families on its waiting list for 30 annual vacancies. By average state secondary school standards, however, 300 is a small school.

Why do schools that want to operate democratically keep their numbers down? The major reason is the nature of relationships in smaller groups. If numbers are low it facilitates the development of democratic procedures and culture in a number of significant ways:

- communication and dialogue are much easier
- consultation, discussion and decision-making are therefore improved
- decisions, although arrived at democratically, can be made quite quickly
- participation can be more direct and more regular
- people feel a sense of ownership and hence responsibility
- responsibility enhances self-discipline rather than imposed discipline
- people know each other better which enables trust to develop
- it creates an informal atmosphere
- smaller numbers help to give students the initial confidence to articulate their views
- it is easier to see people as individuals with differing needs
- the emphasis on the individual necessitates a flexible curriculum with more freedom and more choice

Nevertheless, as was suggested above, although for these reasons smallness can greatly facilitate democratic education, it does not guarantee it. Small schools must also have a philosophy and practice of democratic education. The remainder of this section will examine a series of small schools that have operated democratically in a variety of ways and to a variety of extents. As David Gribble (who teaches as the Sands School described below) has said,

> "That such differences can exist in schools that are united in the extreme forefront of the battle against authoritarian education demonstrates that even when the battle is won, there will be no uniformity"(1994a:3).

The Small School at Hartland, Devon

This school was established in 1982 and caters for 30 secondary level students between ages 11 - 16, and features in a Human Scale Movement video on small schools. It is seen as providing a model for others who deliberately want to establish small schools (Human Scale, 1992). Though not overtly or directly using the language of democracy and democratic education, there is a number of aspects of the school, such as the interpretation of curriculum, teacher - student relationships and the stress on thinking for oneself which sits comfortably with a more democratic approach to learning.

The school rejects the mass production and impersonal nature of large schools and prefers a family model. Education is seen as a partnership between children, teachers and parents. It is also seen holistically with emphasis on active and practical learning as well as intellectual learning and with a major emphasis on relationships with others. This emphasis on the quality of relationships is seen as only really possible in a small school.

The buildings had to be purchased by local shareholders and parents, and charities and trusts have provided money to meet the running costs. There are two full-time teachers working on reduced salaries but parents and other villagers come into the school to help and much use is made of resources in the community.

Originally the curriculum grew from discussion and was agreed with the children and parents, though the school was later forced to adopt aspects of the national curriculum for financial reasons. English, mathematics, science and foreign languages are offered but, despite the national curriculum, the students can also select weekly from a mix of creative and practical activities. Within what is still described as a fluid curriculum the students can choose their own path at their own pace. Knowledge is seen as integrated and networked rather than necessarily divided into 'subjects'. The approach is very child-centred, relationships informal and students are valued as people whose views should be listened to. On the video referred to above one student comments that it is, *"like a family here with everybody pulling together"*

Another comments that you are, *"taught to think for yourself and have ideas of your own"*.

One visiting reporter, Val Hennessy, wrote that she was struck by the atmosphere of bustling diligence and friendly co-operation. She noticed that there were no disgruntled students, no shouting, none of the usual peer group humiliations and none of the usual indignity of having to raise a hand and request to go to the toilet. For her, mutual trust and affection were the qualities that distinguished the school from others.

Sudbury Valley School, Massachusetts

Sudbury Valley School was founded in 1968 and is a private day school financed by student fees, though the tuition fee has always been low by comparison with other private schools in the area. Its numbers vary between sixty and ninety. The school admits anyone who wishes to enrol age 4 to adult, paying no attention to previous school records or other indications of ability or achievement.

Sudbury Valley was founded on a philosophy of democratic values. The primary consideration of those who founded the school was to develop a place where people of all ages can feel comfortable, dignified and free to pursue their own interests. In keeping with this philosophy, the school building is furnished more like a home than an institution, with comfortable chairs predominating and with books not kept in a separate library but along the walls of the rooms that serve many different functions. The school employs a relatively large staff, most of whom are part-time and have careers outside the school. Through this arrangement the school brings many adults with a wide range of interests, skills and knowledge into contact with students at a relatively low cost.

In terms of teaching and learning, the school's most significant feature is the complete absence of a curriculum - there are no academic requirements of any kind. Instead, the initiative for learning is expected to come entirely from the students. Students have no schedules and are assigned to no groups. The school simply leaves them alone to organise their own time and associate with each other and with the staff as they will. Learning therefore takes place in many ways - projects, games, conversations, visits, etc. Staff members teach in this setting mainly through informal conversations and through responding to questions. Learning of a more formal sort also occurs. When students express a desire to pursue a topic systematically with a staff member, a tutorial or course is organised. Sometime staff members initiate seminars and lectures in their fields of interest, but these depend on attracting a sufficient number of participants. Another interesting contrast with other schools is the free association of people of different ages. Age mixing is not only common in informal gatherings but also in formal classes.

Central to the school's educational philosophy is the idea of personal responsibility. Students must generate or discover their own interests, decide what goals to set themselves and decide how to pursue their goals. A corollary is that they must also judge their own progress. The school offers no institutional evaluations - no grades and no written or oral reports of progress. Students will often solicit and receive critiques and judgements but these are personal, not institutional, and are not imposed on students. To receive a high school diploma at Sudbury Valley there is only one requirement. The student must defend a graduation thesis at a meeting open to all members of the school's Assembly, which includes students, staff, trustees, parents and elected public members. Essentially the thesis is that the candidate is ready to take responsibility for him or herself in society at large. Each student has a unique way of presenting and supporting the thesis, which is delivered orally and followed by up to two hours of questions and challenges from the audience. Thesis defences are taken very seriously in the school and most students sit and listen carefully as candidates (whom they know well because of the small size of the school) articulate their arguments as to why they think that they have prepared themselves to participate in the adult world. By the time the student is ready to graduate he or she will have heard many hours of these exchanges and this will play a role in shaping and focusing the student's perception of his or her future as an adult.

The organisation of the school is based on the concept of responsible individuals functioning together on a basis of egalitarianism and open decision-making. The 'School Meeting' consisting of all students and staff has responsibility for administering all of the school's business. Convening once a week and operating on a one person/one vote principle, the School Meeting deals with the entire range of administrative functions including financial management, staff hiring, building and grounds maintenance, public relations, the legislation of all rules of behaviour and the election of clerks and committees to handle the operating details of the school's business. Given the comprehensive nature of the matters covered by the School Meeting and the desire to have everyone involved, it is not surprising that Sudbury Valley needs to operate as a reasonably small school.

In contrast to personal relationships at the school, the School Meeting operates quite formally. A complete agenda is published in advance of the meeting and the standard rules of parliamentary procedure are strictly observed. The meeting's primary goal is efficient, fair and democratic administration of the school. Attendance at the meeting is voluntary and the majority of members tend to show up for matters which concern them directly, though occasional high intensity issues attract a large turnout. Regular attenders are those interested in administration itself or those such as older students with a longer-standing and mature commitment to the school as an institution.

Although the School Meeting is ultimately responsible for handling discipline, it is the 'Judicial Committee' that deals with problems as they arise. This is made up of a chronological cross section of the staff and students and drawn by lot. The committee changes monthly so that everyone serves from time to time. The committee receives and investigates complaints, rules on guilt or innocence and issues sentences. If the committee feels that a situation is particularly serious or intractable it will refer it to the School Meeting. Anyone who feels aggrieved by a sentence may likewise appeal to the meeting. The Judicial Committee is central to the social and moral education that occurs in the school, as here the ethics made explicit in the School Meeting's rules of conduct are applied to real situations.

The school is truly a functioning democracy. Moreover, a longitudinal study of the graduates of Sudbury Valley (on which the above account is primarily based) which looked at what had happened to a sample of 76 students after they had left the school concluded that not only had they not suffered as a result of attending such a school but that they had gone on to good colleges and got good jobs. This was because the school had created in them such traits as a strong sense of responsibility, the ability to take the initiative and solve problems, an ability to communicate effectively and a high commitment to the field in which employment is sought (Gray and Chanoff, 1986).

Sands School, Devon

Sands School is a private school with 30 male and female students aged 11 to 16. The 'head teacher' is David Gribble who was formerly at Dartington Hall School. (The term 'head teacher' is used only for external purposes as legally in Britain there must be one in a school. Inside the school he is known as the 'administrator' because nothing should be decided by one person on the spur of the moment.) Gribble's philosophy is clearly democratic:

> *"There was a time when I put clear limits to the amount of responsibility that I thought should be shared. It now seems clear to me that there are no limits. When they need it children ask for and accept the knowledge that comes from adults' experience. Adults who feel that they have relevant experience that is being ignored can put forward their views for discussion. But what is important is that everyone's opinion should be given weight and taken seriously and that in the end all big decisions should be a joint responsibility. The educational value of such discussions is beyond question enormous, but what is less often accepted, though on reflection it seems just as obvious, is that decisions made as a result of discussion are bound to be better than decisions made without it" (1994b:5).*

The key decision-making body is the School Meeting which takes place weekly. It is chaired by a student, and students and teachers each have a vote. It has complete authority to make decisions about all aspects of school life, many of which are usually regarded as the responsibility of the head teacher. These powers include the appointment and dismissal of staff. The administrator is also appointed by the school meeting. There is also a weekly staff meeting at which the academic or social progress of individual children can be discussed.

All classes in Sands are small and teaching is based on the individual needs of each child. Students and staff have decided that there is a need for organised lessons so there is a fixed, but democratically devised, timetable and students are expected to come to classes, though the final responsibility is given to the student.

Gribble, in reflecting on the nature of Sands School compared with Hadera School in Israel, (discussed below), stressed two ways in which Sands was different:

"The first is that at Sands the care of the grounds, the cooking of lunch, the washing up and all domestic work are done by the students and teachers. This means that the children have real responsibility for their surroundings; they have work to do that has obvious practical implications, and are not surrounded by artificial tidiness created by gardeners and domestic staff.

The second, and I think the more important, is that at Sands there is no system of punishment. At Hadera there is a Discipline Committee that deals with offences and decides on punishments if appropriate; at Sands it is assumed that most people want to behave responsibly and that inconsiderate behaviour is usually regretted; consistent irresponsible behaviour or single serious misdemeanours are dealt with by the school meeting; even then there is hardly ever any punishment" (1994a:3).

Two students from Sands School visited Sudbury Valley in October 1993. The following is one student's account of this visit from one small democratic school to another. As the opening remarks make clear (and to the intrigue of somebody who taught in a school of well over 2,000 students), 'smallness' is very much in the eye and experience of the beholder:

"My first impressions of the place were "Oh my God, this is so BIG". When we first walked in the door, there were little kids running around, which felt very strange as the youngest kid at Sands is 10.

For the first day we sat on the sofa and so many people came up to us and said, "Are you from England?" and, "What's it like?" It was so scary, but after a couple of days we got to know people and settled in really well.

There are a lot of differences between Sudbury Valley and Sands because Sudbury Valley has over 100 students and Sands has only 27. The size was quite overwhelming. The way Sudbury works is more formal, especially the School Meeting.

The School Meetings were always very small; people didn't seem interested in the school which I thought was quite stupid because it's supposed to be their school. The other thing I didn't like about their meetings was that the Chair talked to the kids as though they were business people, not kids. Their School Meetings were good. They were quiet and everyone listened to each other, which doesn't always happen at Sands.

One of the things that I really liked about Sudbury Valley was that the teachers spent a long time with the kids. There were always at least three of them hanging out with the kids, talking or playing games.

There are more rules there. Some of them are really petty and stupid, but most of them are necessary, especially for the younger kids. They also have a thing called a Judicial Council or JC, which is a bit like a mini School Meeting. What happens is that, say one kid hits another, the kid that got hit would fill out a complaint form, saying what had happened. Then in the next JC, five students and one teacher would interview both the children involved and any witnesses and then choose a sentence. The JC happens every day and they pick a new JC committee every month. It works very well and means that you don't have to deal with little complaints in the School Committee. This makes the meeting shorter and more interesting.

The way the school work side is dealt with is very strange. Say if I wanted a lesson, I'd have to find a group of kids (any age) that wanted to do the same subject and arrange a lesson with them. What sometimes happens is that, if you're quite bright, the teachers say that you don't need a lesson, you can pass it yourself, which means that they don't get the attention they need to pass their SATs which are the exams they have in the USA.

At Sudbury Valley, when you want to graduate, you have to do a thing called a piece. This is when the staff members and a lot of the students get together and ask the student that wants to leave questions. Then they look at their behaviour record for the last couple of years and decide whether they're ready to leave or not. If they decide they're allowed to go, the student gets a certificate, which is accepted in the colleges.

I thought Sudbury Valley would be a nice place to go, but I think they could learn a bit from Sands, like making School Meetings more relaxed and cutting down on the school rules. I think Sands should consider having a JC to keep the School Meeting shorter" (Woodward, 1994:6/7).

Hadera School, Israel

The Hadera School differs from the other schools described here in that it is a state school. It was founded in 1987 by a group of parents and educators who worked towards its establishment. It has 300 students from 4-18 years old and includes a nursery, a kindergarten, elementary and high schools and an institute for training teachers. Thus, although internationally 300 is anyway by no means large for a school encompassing secondary level students, Hadera is in fact a number of schools in one.

One of its key goals is to establish a scholastic framework based on respect for human rights without discrimination (which includes discrimination by age within the organisation). The school has taken on the task of applying democratic principles to its educational framework, using democracy as a tool to reach the goal of respecting individual rights within a social framework. In practice this means that the school has four democratic 'authorities': legislative, judicial, executive and comptrolling.

1. The Legislative Authority.

The legislative authority of the school is called 'The Parliament'. Its members consist of all the students, their parents and the school staff. The Parliament meets once a week and is run by a chairperson who is elected once every three months. Any member of Parliament can bring an issue to the floor for discussion.

The Parliamentary meetings determine all school rules, ranging from playground rules to rules governing the acceptance of teachers and students to the school, as well as the allocation of the school budget. Rules are determined according to majority vote by Parliament members present at the deliberations of any particular parliamentary session.

2. The Judicial Authority

The Judicial Authority of the school consists of two committees: the Discipline Committee and the Appeals Committee. Students and teachers are elected to these committees by Parliamentary vote and act as judges. Any person in the school, regardless of age or status, can 'sue', prosecute and be prosecuted using the Disciplinary Committee. When considering a case before the Discipline Committee, its members take into account the seriousness of the offence, hear both sides of the case and, after discussion, give their verdict. In the event that the verdict is not acceptable to one of the disputing sides, the case is referred to the Appeals Committee. This committee functions as the supreme court of the school. After the second hearing of the case, the Appeals Committee gives its verdict. This verdict is final and not subject to further appeal.

3. The Executive Authority

The Executive Authority of the school consists of members of the following committees: Budget Committee, Teachers' Committee,

Student Acceptance Committee, Special Events Committee, Justice and Constitution Committee, School Trips Committee, as well as the heads of various special school functions, i.e. electrical equipment, sanitation, playground, outside connections, etc. All members of the Executive Authority are elected through general elections which are held once a year.

4. The Comptrolling Authority

The school Comptroller and Comptrolling Committee's role is to oversee the function of the executive authority. Investigations can be initiated by the comptroller or result from a formal complaint. The Comptroller is obligated to produce a periodic report which details the results of his/her investigation and his/her personal opinion.

A second key goal of the school is to assist the student in securing the skills necessary to help meet his or her goals. Hadera turns around the standard question of, 'What does my teacher want from me?' Instead, students work with the following questions : 'What am I going to do with the time at my disposal?', 'What are my plans?', 'What are my goals?', 'How will I choose what to do?', 'What should I initiate?', 'How can I be helped and by whom?'. Learning at the Hadera school is based on principles of self-motivation, personal responsibility and personal initiative.

In practice this means that a student is free to plan how to make use of the time he or she has at school with the aid of four main trends of study:

1. Lesson Scheduling: at the beginning of each year an academic schedule is publicised incorporating a wide variety of subjects of study. During the first month of studies, students can audit a course to see if it suits them and from their observations build a lesson plan that meets their needs. There are no required subjects at the school and all lessons are taught under the concept of multi-age, meaning that the lessons are open to all, regardless of age. Each lesson has its own ground-rules (determined by the teacher), and by choosing the course, the student is obliged to abide by those rules.

2. Personal Agreements: A student who does not wish to study within the framework of a classroom can always arrange an independent lesson with a teacher by means of personal agreement. The agreement covers conditions of length of study, frequency of meetings, the students' obligations and the teacher's responsibilities.

3. Study Centres: The school has several study centres which are open all day. Students can work there without the need for prior arrangements with a teacher. The centres are staffed by teachers and are equipped with independent learning material. To date the school has the following learning centres: Hebrew, maths, art, music, theatre, 'lego', movement, social sciences and philosophy, biology, geography, English and science.

4. The Local School Area: The school gives students the opportunity to learn once or twice a week outside of the school campus, based on agreement among the student, his or her parents and the student's Educator (the teacher with an overall responsibility for the student), and can learn with a professional at another institution or in any other experiential work.

Hadera not only has a waiting list of 2,500 families and large numbers of applicants for rarely available teaching posts but also has the full support of the Minister of Education who is seeking to replicate the school in other parts of the country. Having met a group of thoughtful, perceptive and critical students from Hadera at the Sands conference, the writer is not surprised that the Minister is impressed. Moreover, Hadera is an important reminder that in a democratic society small and democratic schools should be available in the state sector for those who wish to attend them.

Summerhill School

The description of Summerhill will be brief because much has been written about it already (see, for example, Lamb 1992; Croall 1983). Summerhill School was founded by A.S. Neill in 1921 in Lyme Regis and moved to Leiston in Suffolk in 1927.

It is perhaps the most famous democratic free school in the world, although some would perhaps use the adjective libertarian rather than democratic. It has about fifty children between the ages of four and sixteen and is financed through fees and donations. Weekly school meetings composed of all staff and students make all decisions about the running of the school. There is a Tribunal which deals with any anti-social behaviour and Ombudsmen who are voluntary arbitrators from amongst the children who try to settle minor problems that might arise. The Ombudsmen change once a fortnight. Students are completely free to choose how they spend their time and no lessons are compulsory though the lessons available are many and varied.

East Midlands Flexi College

The education system of the 21st century is likely to see a radical replacement of the existing authoritarian school by a new kind of school. This will feature flexi-time use of some existing school buildings and new resource centres for use by home-based educating families. The result will be the creation of a regenerated education system in which person-centred learning in democratic and co-operative groupings, enables a wider diversity of provision to meet individuals needs for creative self-development, within the new moral constraints of the current human predicament.

Flexi College is designed to be an adaptable model of such a school. The East Midlands Flexi College has grown out of Philip Toogood's previous 20 years' work in mini-schooled large comprehensives, small schools and community education. A carefully researched proposal was produced in 1991 with Richard Terry, now one of the 4 tutors in the group flexi-teaching partnership working at the flexible learning centre at Monk Street, Tutbury, North Staffordshire. Here parents, teachers, students and local people contract together in an education venture at the heart of which is a small flexible school for students from 8 to 16 years old. In September, a 16 to 19 years group is planned and the Flexi College will be complete when an early childhood section is added later. This cluster of small groups served by a flexi-teaching partnership will be managed by a limited company with charitable status. All such Flexi Colleges will be licensed by a National Foundation for Flexible Learning and will be provided with co-ordination, training and support by the Foundation's directorate. All this will be set up in the next 18 months.

Meanwhile, at East Midlands Flexi College, 17 students and teachers start each day with exercises, a review of world affairs, meetings to plan the day, mornings of intensive small group directed work in Maths, English, Information Technology, and French, afternoons of long autonomous tutor-supported sessions in Art, Design, Expressive Arts, Humanities and Science and finish each day with supported Independent Study sessions. GCSE, 'A' level, GNVQ and NVQ examinations are on offer. The year is framed into 6 modules containing 6 symposium presentation weeks, 3 expeditions and 3 specially negotiated activity weeks. Parents, students, tutors and local people join a Life-long Learning Association. By co-operative work, funds are raised and practical maintenance done. Underpinning the whole development is the informal support and advice provided by the very diverse membership of the Education Now Ltd research, consultancy, and publishing network.

It is called a college because of the contractual basis of membership between tutor and student and vice versa. The bases of this contract are co-operation, self-management and democratic practice. It aims to avoid the setting of learning apart from the community of business, family and everyday life.   Philip Toogood, one of the two tutors at the college, describes a typical day,

"The days are started with half an hour's exercise, incorporating very many different sorts of exercise from Tai Chi to straightforward aerobics. This is followed by a group consideration of the day's news from the early morning Radio 4 recorded broadcast. This is logged and later fed through to a data bank to be used in Humanities studies and for later issue as a digest of interest to young and old locally. A short group meeting then takes place for 15 minutes to make the arrangements for the day and to bring up any urgent points for decision. This is followed by a short break until 10.30.

Supported Independent Study assignments are then undertaken individually or in small groups until lunch, 90 minutes later at midday. Both groups then go out by transport to public play areas, sports centre, public library, tennis club etc. A picnic lunch is eaten wherever the student has gone and the afternoon session begins at 1.30 with a half hour session of writer's workshop, or reader's workshop or numeracy workshop. At 2 p.m. the afternoon activities start (Art, Drama, Design Technology, Humanities or Information Technology). The day ends at 3.45 unless students wish to stay for a further voluntary session. Agreed assignments are continued for homework. During the Independent Studies time on Monday, students have individual tutorials when the assignments are agreed and reviewed. On Fridays between 10.15 and 10.45 the students' logs are reviewed individually with them and a short Tutor Group meeting is held to get ready for the whole school meeting from 10.45 to 11.30. Three or four expeditions are planned and held every year and students run most aspects of these themselves, supported by the tutors. The heart of the whole process is the everyday practice of direct democracy".

In the same paper Toogood quotes Richard Terry, the other tutor at the college, who comments that,

"As a co-operative learning group we are constantly reviewing, criticising and revising our methods, times and practice. However, we do try to maintain a core structure which underpins everything we do, based on the assumption that it is desirable for all students to learn to take responsibility for their own learning. This does not happen overnight, nor with the greatest of ease; on the contrary, it requires hard, often stressful, work. Also required are: a readiness to accept and adapt to change, and above all the careful nurturing of a set of relationships based on mutual respect and trust" (Toogood, 1995:85/6).

Chapter four

Conclusion

Small schools are an international phenomenon, especially in rural areas. While the evidence that they are more expensive than large schools is ambivalent there is considerable evidence to suggest that academically they can perform as well as large schools, that they are popular with students, staff and parents, that they play an important part in the survival of rural communities and that they are less prone to problems of alienation, deviance and disruption. Moreover, well organised and managed small schools can provide as wide a curriculum as large schools. Their advocates argue that the quality of relationships possible in education 'on a human scale' can make them a more cost-effective way to provide education and at the very least they ought to be an option available to all parents within the state system as well as for those who can afford to send their children to private schools.

It is, however, recognised that small schools can face potential problems in regard to resources and isolation. A well managed small school will often therefore consider membership of a cluster in which they can retain their independence and identity but gain through co-operation with other small schools. Governments world-wide have recognised the importance of small schools and many are now encouraging and supporting school clusters. Conversely, historically created large schools do not necessarily have to stay that way. Mini-schooling offers an interesting and viable alternative to the monolithically organised school of 1,000 plus students.

For this writer, however, the nub of the effectiveness argument in relation to small schools lies with democracy. One criticism of the whole school-effectiveness literature is that it tries to be neutral about the question of goals. However, in judging effectiveness it is important to ask the prior questions of 'effective at what and for what?' Democracy is a much espoused aim in education but only rarely has educational practice matched the rhetoric. Yet, in societies which claim to be democratic or which are aiming to become democratic, can a school be described as effective if it is not contributing to democratic skills and values? If education for democracy is to be other than an empty phrase then schools must be organised according to democratic principles, though, as this book has made clear, this is very far from meaning uniformity in democratic practice.

Small schools can provide the direct experience of everyday democracy in action that is more difficult in larger schools. Indeed, the better human relationships that small schools claim to foster could easily turn out be benevolent, kindly and caring authoritarianism if the issue of democratic organisation and practices is not deliberately and directly addressed. Small schools have an important part to play in the development of more democratic and flexible human beings in the future but their size will not automatically guarantee them this role.

References

Anderson, J. (1991) 'Death of the dinosaurs?', in Toogood, P. (Ed.) **Small Schools** (Ticknall: Education Now).

Atkins, V. and Rivers, M. (1994) 'Clustering - what's in it for us?', **Management in Education** 8, 1.

Banks, M. et al (1992) **Careers and Identities** (Milton Keynes: Open University Press).

Bray, M. (1987a) **Are Small Schools the Answer?** (London: Commonwealth Secretariat).

Bray, M. (1987b) **School Clusters in the Third World : Making them Work** (Paris: UNESCO).

Bray, M. with Lillis, K. (Eds.) (1988) **Community Financing of Education** (Oxford: Pergamon Press).

Brock-Utne, B., Appiah-Endresen, I. and Oliver, C. (1994) **Evaluation of the NAMAS Support to Mweshipandeka Senior Secondary School** (Windhoek: Namibia Association of Norway).

Brown, C. (1995) 'Methods in political education', **Citizenship** 4, 2.

Burstall, C. (1974) **Primary French in the Balance** (Slough: National Foundation for Educational Research).

Campbell, W. (1980) 'School size : its influence on pupils', in Fitch, A. and Scrimshaw, P. (Eds.) **Standards, Schooling and Education** (London: Hodder and Stoughton).

Conway, M. and Damico, S. (1993) 'Facing up to multiculturalism: Means as ends in democratic education', paper delivered to the International Conference on Education for Democracy in a Multicultural Society, Jerusalem, Israel.

Croall, J. (1983) **Neill of Summerhill** (London: Routledge and Kegan Paul).

Davies, L. and Harber, C. (forthcoming) **School Management and School Effectiveness in Developing Countries** (London: Cassell).

De la Cour, P. (1988) 'Diversity in one country: the Danish example', **Education Now News and Review** May/June 1988.

Dneprov, E. (1995) 'Background to the reform and new policies in education in Russia', in Chapman,J., Froumin, I., and Aspin, D. (Eds.) **Creating and Managing the Democratic School** (London: The Falmer Press).

Department for Education (1993) **Good Management in Small Schools** (London: DFE).

Dimmock, C. (1995) 'Building democracy in a school setting : The principal's role', in Chapman, J., Froumin, I., and Aspin, D. (Eds.) **Creating and Managing the Democratic School** (London: The Falmer Press).

Dunstan, J. (1995) 'The structure of democracy in educational settings: The relationship between the school and the system', in Chapman, J., Froumin, I., and Aspin, D. (Eds.) **Creating and Managing the Democratic School** (London: The Falmer Press).

Edington, E. and Gardner, C. (1984) 'The relationship of school size to scores in the affective domain from the Montana testing service examination', **Education** 105.

Edmonds, E. (1989) 'Small schools', **RSA Journal** September 1989.

Edmonds, E. and Besai, F. (1977) 'Small schools', **Head Teachers Review** 68.

Ehman, L. (1980) 'The American high school in the political socialisation process', **Review of Educational Research** 50.

Etzioni, A. (1995) **The Spirit of Community: Rights, Responsibilities and the Communitarian Agenda** (New York: Harper Collins).

Farrant, J. (1986) **Improving the Cost-Effectiveness of Small Schools** (London: Commonwealth Secretariat).

Francis, L. (1992) 'Primary school size and pupil attitudes : small is happy?', **Educational Management and Administration** 20, 2.

Fullan, M. (1991) **The New Meaning of Educational Change** (London: Cassell).

Galton, M. and Patrick, H. (1990) **Curriculum Provision in the Small Primary School** (London: Routledge).

Gray, P. and Chanoff, D. (1986) 'Democratic schooling: what happens to young people who have charge of their own education?', **American Journal of Education** 94, 2.

Gribble, D. (1994a) 'Comparing Sands School with other democratic schools', **Education Now News and Review** Winter/Spring 1994.

Gribble, D. (1994b) **Hadera Conference Journal** 2, February 1994.

Harber, C. (1990) 'Anti-racism and political education for democracy', in Hoskin, M., and Sigel R. (Eds.) **Education for Democratic Citizenship in Multi-Ethnic Societies** (New Jersey: Lawrence Erlbaum).

Harber, C. (1992) 'Effective and ineffective schools: an international perspective on the role of research', **Educational Management and Administration** 20, 3.

Harber, C. (1993a) 'Prismatic society revisited : theory and educational administration in developing countries', **Oxford Review of Education** 19, 4.

Harber, C. (1993b) 'Democratic management and school effectiveness in Africa: Learning from Tanzania', **Compare** 23, 3.

Harber, C. (1995) (Ed.) **Developing Democratic Education** (Ticknall: Education Now).

Harber, C. and Meighan, R. (1989) **The Democratic School** (Ticknall: Education Now).

Hattersley, A. (1936) **More Annals of Natal** (Pietermaritzburg: Shuter and Shooter).

Heal, K. (1978) Misbehaviour among school children: the role of the school in strategies of prevention', **Policy and Politics** 6.

Hemming, J. (1991) 'Size matters', in Toogood, P. (Ed.) **Small Schools** (Ticknall: Education Now).

Hepburn, M. (1984) 'Democratic schooling - five perspectives from research', **International Journal of Political Education** 6.

Hodgetts, C. (1995) 'Human scale in New York', **Human Scale Education News,** December 1995.

Hopkins, D. (1985) 'Leadership in the smaller primary school: dilemmas and decisions related to mixed age range classes', in Hopkins, D. **Leadership in the Primary School** (Swansea: West Gamorgan Institute of Higher Education).

Hopkins, D. and Ellis, P. (1991) 'The effective small primary school : some significant factors', **School Organisation** 11, 1.

Howells, R. (1982) **Curriculum Provision in the Small Primary School** (Cambridge: Cambridge Institute of Education).

Human Scale Movement (1986) **Newsletter** No. 1.

Human Scale Movement (1992) **Education on a Human Scale** (Plymouth: Coleridge Video and Teaching Pack).

Jensen, K. and Walker, S. (1989) **Towards Democratic Schooling: European Experiences** (Milton Keynes: Open University Press).

John, P. and Osborn, A. (1992) 'The influence of school ethos on pupils' citizenship attitudes', **Educational Review** 44, 2.

Kohl, H. (1970) **The Open School** (London: Methuen).

Lamb, A. (1992) **The New Summerhill** (Harmondsworth: Penguin).

Lynch, J. (1992) **Education for Citizenship in a Multicultural Society** (London: Cassell).

McGurk, H. (1987) **What Next?** (London: Economic and Social Research Council).

Meighan, R. (1986) **A Sociology of Educating** (2nd edition, London: Cassell).

Meighan, R. (1992) 'Small schooling', in Meighan,R. and Toogood, P. **Anatomy of Choice in Education** (Ticknall: Education Now).

Meighan, R. (1994) **The Freethinkers' Guide to the Educational Universe** (Nottingham: Educational Heretics Press).

Meighan, R. (1995) **The Freethinkers' Pocket Directory to the Educational Universe** (Nottingham: Educational Heretics Press).

Mortimore, R., Sammons, P , Stoll, L., Lewis, D. and Ecob, R. (1988) **School Matters** (Salisbury: Open Books).

Munro, I. (1975) 'The case for the small rural school', **Education in the North** 12.

Nagel, T. (1992) **Quality Between Tradition and Modernity: Patterns of Cognition in Zimbabwe** (Pedagogisk Forskningsinstitutt, University of Oslo).

Nash, R. (1977) **Conditions of Learning in Rural Primary Schools** (London: Social Science Research Council).

Nash, R. (1980) **Schooling in Rural Societies** (London: Methuen).

Patrick, H. and Hargreaves, L. (1990) 'Small and large schools: some comparisons' in Galton, M. and Patrick, H. **Curriculum Provision in the Small Primary School** (London: Routledge).

Potter, A. and Williams, M. (1994) 'Clustering in small primary schools: an organisational case', **School Organisation** 14, 2.

Reid, K., Hopkins, D. and Holly, P. (1987) **Towards the Effective School** (Oxford: Blackwell).

Richmond, J. (1992) 'The concept of the small secondary school', **Educational Studies** 18, 3.

Robinson, N. and Koehn, D. (1994) 'Student councils in primary schools: contributors to management decisions?', **Management in Education** 8, 1.

Schools Council (1975) **Small Schools Study** (Unpublished paper quoted in Hopkins and Ellis Op. Cit.)

Shipman, M. (1971) **Education and Modernisation** (London: Faber).

Starkey, H. (1991) (Ed.) **Teaching About Human Rights** (Strasbourg: Council of Europe).

Stiles, R. (1986) 'Snuffing out small schools!', **Human Scale Newsletter 1.**

Tesfamariam, T. (1993) **Democratic School Practice in Eritrea** (Unpublished Certificate of Education Essay, University of Birmingham).

Thorpe, T. (1994) 'Teacher training in human rights and democracy in Russia', **Citizenship** 3, 2.

Tomlinson, J. (1990) **Small, Rural and Effective** (Institute of Education, University of Warwick).

Toogood, P. (1991) 'Introduction' in Toogood, P. (Ed.) **Small Schools** (Ticknall: Education Now).

Toogood, P. (1992) 'Minischooling', in Meighan, R. and Toogood, P. **Anatomy of Choice in Education** (Ticknall: Education Now).

Toogood, P. (1995) 'Minischooling as democratic practice', in Harber, C. (Ed.) **Developing Democratic Education** (Ticknall: Education Now).

Tsang, M. and Wheeler, C. (1993) 'Local initiatives and their implications for a multi-level approach to school improvement in Thailand', in Levin, H. and Lockheed, M. (Eds.) **Effective Schools in Developing Countries** (London: The Falmer Press).

Vulliamy, G. (1987) 'School effectiveness research in Papua New Guinea', **Comparative Education** 23, 2.

Webb, R. (1993) 'Small schools and the national curriculum', **Report** November 1993.

Woodward, J. (1994) 'Visit to Sudbury Valley', **Hadera Conference Journal** 2, February 1994.